The
KIDS' MONEY
Book

The KIDS' MONEY Book

EARNING, SAVING, SPENDING, INVESTING, DONATING

Jamie Kyle McGillian

STERLING CHILDREN'S BOOKS
New York

To Geno, because money comes and goes, but true
love sticks around. And to Bailey and Devan, who cost
me a lot of dough!

STERLING CHILDREN'S BOOKS
New York

An Imprint of Sterling Publishing Co., Inc.
1166 Avenue of the Americas
New York, NY 10036

STERLING CHILDREN'S BOOKS and the distinctive Sterling Children's Books
logo are trademarks of Sterling Publishing Co., Inc.

ISBN 978-1-4549-1977-3

Library of Congress Cataloging-in-Publication Data
McGillian, Jamie Kyle
The kids' money book : earning, saving, spending, investing, donating
/ Jamie Kyle McGillian ; illustrated by Ian Phillips.
p. cm.
Includes index.
Summary: Introduces how to manage money, from earning an allowance to
budgeting to saving for college.
ISBN 0-8069-8223-3
Children—Finance, Personal—Juvenile literature. 2. Finance, Personal—Juvenile
literature. [1. Finance, Personal. 2. Money.]
Phillips, Ian, ill. II. Title.
HG179 .M238 2003
332.024′054—dc21
2002015506

Distributed in Canada by Sterling Publishing
c/o Canadian Manda Group, 664 Annette Street
Toronto, Ontario, Canada M6S 2C8
Distributed in the United Kingdom by GMC Distribution Services
Castle Place, 166 High Street, Lewes, East Sussex, England BN7 1XU

For information about custom editions, special sales, and premium and
corporate purchases, please contact Sterling Special Sales at 800-805-5489
or specialsales@sterlingpublishing.com.

Manufactured in China

Lot #:
2 4 6 8 10 9 7 5 3 1
06/16

www.sterlingpublishing.com

Illustrations by Jane Sanders
Design by Lorie Pagnozzi

Contents

Introduction

hirteen years ago when I first wrote *The Kids' Money Book*, I had two little spenders at home. In those days, my daughters were spending their pocket money on candy and costume jewelry—money wasn't very complicated to them.

Now my two little spenders are teens. They still buy candy from time to time, but they spend much of their money on coffee drinks or snacks when they're hanging out with friends. They also buy music on iTunes and apps for their phones. Money is very important to them. As a result, they are always looking for ways to make a few bucks. I try to encourage them to save and to not always spend every dollar that's in their pockets.

In the past decade, as my little spenders have grown into big spenders, the world of money has changed, thanks to technology. When the first edition of this book came out in 2003, there were no Facebook, Instagram, or Twitter, no iPhones, no Netflix. Many of you probably cannot even imagine that! As these things have come onto the scene, they've brought about changes in what we buy and how we pay. So we've updated this book to present you with the latest word on saving, spending, earning, investing, and donating.

As you get older, money becomes more important to you. You will need it to get an education, rent an apartment, buy a house, take a vacation, travel to a job, and maybe even get married.

Whoa, let's not get ahead of ourselves! Most young people are not yet paying their own rent, but they are consumers, or people who are spending money. So what are they buying?

TEEN SPENDING

A study called "Taking Stock with Teens" was conducted by Piper Jaffray, an investment bank, in 2015. It reflected the opinions of more than six thousand teens from forty-four US states. The study found that teens spend more of their cash on food than anything else; it accounts for almost 23 percent of teen spending. Teens are spending money at these restaurants, and in this order:

1. Starbucks   3. Chick-fil-A

2. Chipotle   4. Panera Bread

Teens also spend about 20 percent of their money on clothing, at these stores:

1. Nike   3. American Eagle

2. Forever 21   4. Ralph Lauren

According to the study, teens often buy things online.

You may not be a teen yet, but you will be in the not-so-distant future. How will you spend your money? Will you spend your cash on iced lattes and burritos, or will you invest in your future? Will you make smart money choices?

Most teens like to spend money, but during hard times, they may cut back on their spending. It's the same with adults. In good times, people may spend money on meals, movies, or shows. But when times are not so good, people may stay home. In order to really understand this, it's important to look at the economy, or the system of how money is made and used.

In 2008, there was a recession. What happens in a recession? Well, buying, selling, and production slow down or stop. Unable to sell their products or services, companies often have to lay off workers. That means the unemployment rate rises.

Without jobs, many people can't pay their bills. Many homeowners lose their homes. Some families learn how to survive with less money. They may move to smaller homes. Some workers find a few part-time jobs to make up for one lost job.

The recession left the economy in a weakened state. We are still feeling its effects today, but economists, the people who study the economy, believe that it is just one part of the business cycle. Basically, that means what goes down will eventually go up again—even if financial experts say that it is taking a while for us to recover.

All the more reason to be extra smart about money.

1

Moments in Money

You don't need money for everything. Some things are free: air, water, sunsets, moonlight, rainbows, snowflakes, beaches. But without money, how would we get our homes, cars, phones, clothing, treats, and books? Thousands of years ago, there was no money. So how did people survive?

A HISTORY OF MONEY

Long ago, when people needed things that others had, they bartered; that's another word for trading. If you've ever traded baseball cards with a friend, you have bartered. You got what you wanted or needed in exchange for something else.

Think of how life would be now if every time you needed or wanted something, you had to swap for it: "I'll give you this sweater for those shoes." "I'll give you two pillows for a blanket." Every time you got something, you would have to give up something. Your exchanges would depend on your needs and how much you had, as well as what the other person wanted to give in exchange.

Bartering had its problems. What if, for example, you wanted food, but you had nothing that the trader wanted? Or what if you needed water or medicine very badly, but the trader would take only cattle and animal skins in exchange—which you also needed? If the person you were trading with knew how desperate you were for the water or the medicine, he might not make a trade unless you paid a lot (like all your cattle or animal skins!). It might not have been easy to find a third party to come and help you determine if the trade was fair. Imagine the arguments that some people had over their trades back then . . . and maybe still do today somewhere in the world.

And just imagine what it would have been like to travel on foot with all your wares, eager to make a trade but tired of hauling around all that stuff. You'd probably be thinking, "There's gotta be a better way."

In some ways we still barter today. What if you can't get Wi-Fi from where you are, but you really need to hook up to the Internet? You might consider going to a café that offers free Wi-Fi services. You buy a drink and a snack in exchange for some uninterrupted Wi-Fi time. Sounds like a pretty fair trade.

But bartering as a system didn't last.

THE ORIGIN OF MONEY

The idea of a medium of exchange, which was a common measure of value, came onto the scene. Depending on where you lived, the agreed-upon medium of exchange might be salt, animal skins, feathers, beads, or corn. Or it could be amber, eggs, ivory, cattle, seashells, tea, fish hooks, fur, and even tobacco. Cattle were one of the first and oldest forms of money. With a medium of exchange, there was something to count. It gave us a value system that we could all agree on.

But, of course, there were problems with some of these early forms of money. Cattle were too heavy to travel with. Certain forms of money, such as eggs and corn, would rot, and tea and tobacco would blow away. Most of these forms of money would not fit in your wallet!

That's when people began to realize that they needed some sort of "thing" that had an agreed-upon value to everyone. Something small that would be easy to carry and that would last . . .

From coins to paper

Precious metals, like gold and silver, came to be used as money. Lydia, an ancient kingdom in what is now known as Turkey, was the first country to use gold to make money. To honor King Croesus of Lydia, the gold coins were stamped with a lion's head. As coins became popular in other countries, pictures of their leaders were stamped on the faces of the coins.

Why were metal coins such a success?

* Coins could be different—one coin had one value, another had another value.
* Coins went wherever you went and were easy to carry.
* Coins didn't wear out, rot, or run away.
* Coins could be limited in number, but enough could be made so that they wouldn't run out.
* Coins could be melted down to make new money.

The first metal money was used about 4,500 years ago. Use of the metal money soon began to spread through Europe and the Middle East. Then, about 1,800 years ago, the Chinese invented paper money. The paper represented an amount of money and could be redeemed for something valuable, like gold. The paper money was much lighter to carry than the heavy coins, and it was also much cheaper to make.

Ancient temples were the first banks. They were considered the safest place to store money because people believed that nobody would steal from a place of worship.

As travel between cities began to expand, and people began to trade more freely with other cultures, some traders began to pay people to exchange coins from other cities; these people took a fee from the money they exchanged. Called "money changers," they were the first known bankers.

THE NEW MONEY

Money has evolved over time for our convenience. Some people don't even carry cash these days. They use online services or apps to transfer money from one person to another, from one place to another. These services send, receive, and request money for you. Almost anybody can do it, as long as they have a bank account. People also use credit cards and debit cards to pay for things by drawing money directly out of their bank accounts.

Electronic services make it a snap to pay the bills. Just think, if you owed someone $50 and you only had a $100 bill in your pocket, you would have to first break the bill in order to pay the person. With electronic money, you don't have to give that a thought. Paying a bill is as easy as sending an e-mail or text. Can you imagine paper money and coins becoming a thing of the past?

Bitcoin is trending

Bitcoin is a type of cryptocurrency. It exists only in the virtual world. You can't put these coins in your pocket. And you can't buy bitcoins from a bank. With bitcoins, two parties exchange money without the bank knowing about it or taking a share of it. Created in 2009, bitcoins were designed to take away power from banks and government. But using bitcoins can cause other problems. For instance, without a written transaction from a bank, how can you prove that you actually paid for something? There is some debate about whether bitcoin is officially a currency or a commodity; the US government currently classifies it as a commodity.

Bitcoins are stored in an online "wallet." What that really means is an account that has been set up on a website. Transactions happen only in an online market, and users cannot be traced.

Bitcoins can be used to buy different things, but the catch is, the seller has to accept them, and to date, most businesses do not. However, bitcoins can be used at some major stores and even some online services. You can also use bitcoins to pay for space travel, just in case you were planning a trip to the moon.

Some kids throughout the world are already using bitcoins to buy online games, such as WoozWorld, or stuff from Amazon or Dell. The popular game Minecraft has incorporated bitcoins as a way of teaching young people about digital currency.

Some people think that bitcoins are the way of the future. Some kids are even getting their allowance in bitcoins! Other people think that this form of cryptocurrency is just a trend that will fade. What do you think?

From tea leaves to coins, from notes to plastic and bitcoins, the face of money continues to change.

Money Timeline

Money didn't happen overnight. The idea of money, and then the making and different uses of it, took thousands of years to develop. Here's a quick timeline to bring you up to date.

Note: Dates up to the year 1331 are circa, meaning "approximate."

9000–6000 BCE

Cattle and crops are used as money. Cattle are the oldest known form of money.

1200 BCE

Mollusks called "cowries" are used as currency in China.

687 BCE

First coins are invented in Lydia, Asia Minor.

600–570 BCE

Coin usage spreads from Lydia to Greece. Before this, the Athenians used iron nails as money.

118 BCE

Leather money is introduced into China. It consists of pieces of white deerskin with colorful borders.

200 CE

Paper money is invented in China.

1160–1200 CE

Wooden sticks, or tallies, are used as credit receipts in England. Notches representing a certain amount of money are cut into the stick. The stick is then split down the middle, one part serving as a receipt for the creditor, the other a reminder for the debtor, who owes the amount.

1232–1253 CE

Gold coins are issued by several Italian states.

1236 CE

The Mongol Empire issues paper money.

1319–1331 CE

Parts of India and Japan issue paper money.

1440 CE

The modern press is invented by the printer Johannes Gutenberg.

1452–1519 CE

The first milled coins are made using the designs of artist Leonardo da Vinci and a water-driven mill.

1500 ＊ POTLATCH

1535 ＊ WAMPUM

1566	In England, the Royal Exchange is built, demonstrating the importance of banking.
1599	Pepper becomes a valued commodity, sometimes worth more than its weight in gold. The Dutch try to corner the pepper market.
1702	 Sir Isaac Newton, director of the England's Royal Mint, assays the value of fifty-six different foreign silver and gold coins (finding the percentage of impurities in precious metal) relative to the British standard.
1715	Due to British coinage shortages, in North Carolina and other parts of North America wampum, tobacco, and other natural resources are used as money substitutes.
1793	The US Mint begins making money for circulation, producing 11,178 copper pennies.
1848	The California Gold Rush results in a massive increase in the production of gold coins.

DID YOU KNOW?

Potlatch (the origin of "potluck") festivities were one of the customs of the native peoples of the American Northwest. The ceremonial occasion consisted of dancing, feasting, and an elaborate gift exchange of expensive fabrics, jewelry, and other priceless items where the tribes and participants tried to outdo each other. At some point, laws were passed and the extravagant, traditional gift giving was stopped.

The best-known form of money among Native Americans was wampum, made from clamshells. Strings of the beads were used for money as well as ornamentation by many North American Indians. The Indian word "wampum" means "white," the color of the beads. By 1637, the Massachusetts Bay Colony had declared wampum to be legal tender (OK to be used as money).

1909

Abraham Lincoln's image is put on the new American penny, marking the one hundredth anniversary of his birth.

1929

A massive stock market crash on Black Monday causes billions of dollars to disappear from the American economy and four thousand banks to fold.

1992

A single European market is set up to lift barriers to capital, labor, goods, and services.

2002

The euro replaces the national coinages of twelve European countries.

2008

Recession hits the United States, as well as the rest of the globe.

2009

Bitcoin is created.

Many of today's coins have milled, or ridged, edges. Putting ridges around coins started long ago, when coins were made of gold and silver. Certain people at that time would secretly shave pieces off the edges of the coins—and sell the shavings! Ridges became part of the manufacture of coins made with precious metals to stop the thieves.

A MONEY STORY TO YAP ABOUT

Hundreds of years ago, the natives of Yap in the South Pacific solved the problem of stolen money—no one could snatch coins that weighed close to a thousand pounds!

Yap money rocks, made of limestone, often weighed five hundred pounds and were hammered and scraped into shape. A hole was then drilled by hand through the center of each money rock so it could be moved or carried by placing a long heavy pole through the center. The stones were moved to the island of Yap from the island of Palau, some 250 miles away. The islanders would travel to Palau in open canoes and ferry the stones back on wooden rafts.

Acquiring the large stones was difficult and dangerous, but Yap tradition and culture placed great importance on the hard work of actually "making money."

2

Money Matters

How much does money matter to you, and how sensible are you with it? Will you be the kind of person who always looks like you're made of money? Will you always be on the way to, or on the way back from, hard-to-pronounce places that specialize in incredible sunsets and palm trees? Or are your needs simpler? Are you happy with a small home, a used car, and a nice meal at a restaurant every now and then?

Test your money sense—your making and spending skills—with this quiz. There are no right or wrong answers, only wise and not-so-wise choices about money. When you're done, add up your score. What have you learned about yourself?

QUIZ TIME!

THE MONEY SENSE QUIZ

1. You just heard a new song. You love it so much, you . . .

   a. buy it on iTunes.

   b. buy every song the band ever recorded.

   c. check to see if the song is on a streaming service.

   d. beg your friend to buy it so it won't cost you a dime.

2. You find $20 in a shoe in your closet. You . . .

   a. put ten bucks in the bank and the other ten in your wallet.

   b. treat all your friends to snacks.

   c. put it in your college fund.

   d. hide it between the couch cushions for a rainy day.

3. You try on a new pair of jeans that fit great. Only trouble is, they cost an arm and a leg. You . . .

   a. buy them right away.

   b. check back with the store every day to see if they have gone on sale.

   c. look online to see if you can find the same jeans at a better price.

   d. ask your grandma to buy them for you. Maybe she will throw in sneakers, too.

4. You and a buddy are throwing a surprise party for a friend. You . . .

a. chip in with your bud to buy food, drinks, balloons, a cake, and a gift.

b. buy everything with your allowance, including a karaoke machine—after all, your friend only turns ten once.

c. ask your friend's parents to foot the bill for everything. They *are* really rich.

d. save money by chipping in with your bud for a pizza, serving water instead of juice or soda, and baking a cake instead of buying one.

5. You hear about a charity that you like. You want to contribute, so you . . .

a. ask your parents for money to give to the charity.

b. volunteer your time every day at the charity headquarters.

c. participate in a walkathon fund-raiser and make a donation from your own pocket.

d. put the name of the charity in your future donations file.

6. You've been saving up to buy an electric guitar. When you're ready, you . . .

a. buy the best one. You deserve it.

b. buy the cheapest one and give yourself a pat on the back for saving money.

c. buy one secondhand that's well made and has all the features you want at a competitive price.

d. ask your parents to buy it for you and promise them that you will practice at least once a month.

SCORING

Add up your score. Here are the point values for each response.

1. a=3, b=1, c=4, d=2   **3.** a=2, b=3, c=4, d=1   **5.** a=2, b=3, c=4, d=1

2. a=4, b=2, c=3, d=1   **4.** a=3, b=2, c=1, d=4   **6.** a=3, b=2, c=4, d=1

Scorecard

6–8 points ✳
Needs Improvement

Open your eyes and start thinking about how money affects you and those around you. Start by playing a few rounds of Monopoly. Keep track of your money. Invest in a piggy bank, and start saving!

9–12 points ✳
Room to Grow

Learn from your money mistakes. Everyone makes them, but smart people learn from them. Set money goals. Save a week's allowance each month. Earn extra bucks in creative ways. Start thinking about setting up a college fund today.

13–18 points ✳
Real Potential

You are on your way! Get out into the community and ask people for their best money advice. Compile your own money book by gathering advice from all the money mavens you've spoken to, as well as articles and books you've read. Nurture those money skills. Explore the idea of saving for a rainy day.

19–23 points ✳
Impressive Money Style

You are on your way to genuine money smarts. Team up with a friend and set up your own business. Try your hands at odd jobs. Collect a jar of lucky pennies and use it to cover business expenses.

24 points ✳
Total Money Brains

You are a money mogul headed for real financial success. Read money publications in your spare time. Record your best money ideas in a journal; maybe even blog about it. Do something great, like raise money for your local children's hospital by producing a talent show. Become known for your money smarts!

About your answers:

1. Nurture Your Own Interests in Responsible Ways.

The best answer here is **c** because it reflects a smart attitude about spending. Of course, if you are a true music lover, there is no harm in buying the song. However, buying every song the band ever recorded is kind of extreme, don't you think?

2. Make Solid Decisions that Reflect Good Judgment.

The best answer is **a**, because you are saving half the money and preparing to spend the other half. There's no need to put it all in the college fund at your age. Treating your friends to snacks may make you popular, but the more you do it, the more they will expect it. And what good will hiding the money in the couch cushions do you?

3. Put a Price on Fashion and Ask Yourself—Is It Worth It?

If you really love those jeans, go out and buy them. But if they are expensive, it is best to think about the purchase. The best answer is **c**, which is called comparison shopping. You never know when you are going to find a sale on the Internet or at the mall. Asking Grandma to buy the pants for you isn't taking responsibility for your own wants.

4. Be Generous and Kind and Reap the Rewards.

You are a good friend to throw a party for another friend. But watch out, this can get expensive. Nobody expects you to cash out your bank account. Choice **d** is smart because you can scale down the party and ask friends to help. But it's not your friend's parents' place to help unless they offer.

5. Be Charitable from the Heart.

Being charitable is a wonderful trait. The contribution that you are making should come from your own pocket, but you should also put some of your time into the cause. Choice **c** is smartest, and you will see that finding a way to become involved *and* to contribute to the cause will give you a feeling of true satisfaction.

6. **Don't Be Impulsive with Expensive Items.**

An electric guitar, huh? That's a serious purchase. You don't want to get the absolute cheapest one, or it might break easily. You don't need the finest one unless you are a professional musician. You just need a good one that you can learn on. Choice **c** is intelligent because a vintage guitar with a great sound will last a long time. And isn't it awesome that you bought it yourself with no help from the 'rents?

WHERE DOES IT ALL GO?

A few bucks on a decaf espresso, a video game, a burrito here and there, a tube of hair gel, some movie tickets, and you are out of funds.

Get wise about money while you're still young! If you wait until you're grown up to think about how to make and save money, it could end up costing you a fortune. Start thinking about it now, while you're still a kid, and maybe you'll be on the right track to a successful financial future.

Which is more costly?

Making money mistakes when you're a kid (like running out of allowance and going without a snack or the latest nail polish) or making serious money mistakes when you're a grown-up (like losing your car because you can't make the payments, and the bank taking your house)? Grown-ups who don't learn money sense while they are young often learn the hard way.

Even if they do avoid big money mistakes, always worrying about paying bills and not having enough money to take care of the family are not fun.

Learn now to make smart money decisions and you'll have a better chance of leading the kind of life that you want to.

What's in your future?

Imagine you're a grown-up. What role will money play in your life? What if you want to be a writer, but you know a writing career will not make you rich? Will you be happy writing but living in a small apartment with few extravagances? When you think of home sweet home, are you seeing a mansion or a tiny house? Do you believe that you could live anywhere and be happy as long as you are doing something you love? Think about what you may want to do when you grow up. Then find out what the average salary is for that job. Talk with your parents or other adults about what kind of life that job affords you. Does it fit with who you are? How will you spend the money you earn? Maybe you love turtles. Start saving now for that awesome trip to the Galápagos Islands before college.

KNOW THE DIFFERENCE
BETWEEN NEEDS AND WANTS

How do you know the best way to spend a few bucks? Is it better to use the money to go out with friends for lunch, or to buy a couple of good books for your personal library? Which purchase is more practical, and which one will provide you with more enjoyment?

Everyone has his or her own way of deciding what to buy or not buy. We are all different, but we all have to separate the things we need from the things we want.

Learning the difference between what we need and what we want is a huge step toward learning to use money wisely. What's the difference between your needs and your wants? Your needs are the things you must have—food, clothing, and shelter. Your wants are the things that you wish you had—concert tickets, an upgraded cell phone, those trendy new sneakers everyone else has.

Go through the list below and mark each item with an *N* for need or a *W* for want.

_____ three square meals a day

_____ an awesome movie collection

_____ medicine

_____ a shopping spree at the mall

_____ eyeglasses or contact lensesw

_____ a new outfit

_____ expensive sneakers

_____ school supplies

_____ a puppy

_____ socks and underwear

_____ fancy chocolates

_____ a credit card

_____ a cell phone

_____ a computer

NEED

WANT

It's all right to have a lot of wants, but the idea is to keep them in check. Think of your wants as ice-cream sundaes. What would happen if every time you wanted a sundae, you had one? You'd probably get really sick of sundaes! But if you limit the number of times you treat yourself, when you do have a sundae: mmm, is that good!

Just as no two people are the same, no two people have exactly the same needs and wants. And these needs and wants often change. What are some of your needs and wants?

Keep a monthly record. Notice how your needs and wants change. Something high on your list now may drop to the bottom by next year. As you mature, and as your environment changes, your needs and wants change, too.

Keep your wants in check by making a pact with yourself not to buy anything on your want list for an entire month. After the month is up, review your list. What can you cross off the list? If you can't make it a month, try starting out with a week.

Add up the cost of all the items on your want list. How much money do you save if you don't give in?

ADJUST YOUR ATTITUDE—MONEY CAN'T BUY YOU LOVE

Money can buy you all sorts of things, but it can't give you a shining personality. It can't make you strong. (In fact, it can reveal your weaknesses!)

So is money a good thing or a bad thing? That depends. Take a look at the two sides of money.

MONEY IS COOL WHEN:

* You earn it from doing hard work.
* You spend it on someone other than yourself.
* It brings you together with old or new friends.
* You buy something that brings you true joy.
* You win it.
* You use it to help someone.
* You find some in the pocket of your old jean jacket.
* You're way under budget.

MONEY IS UNCOOL WHEN:

* You lose it.

* You've spent it all, even your lunch money.

* Someone owes you some.

* You owe someone else some.

* You fight over it with friends or a sibling.

* Someone brags about how much he or she has.

* You're way over your budget.

* You spend all your time trying to get more.

Money is personal

When John D. Rockefeller was the richest man in the world, he was asked, "How much money is enough?" His reply was, "Just a little more."

How do you feel about those crisp bills and shiny coins? How important is having money to you? Do you think it's the key to happiness? Does it really measure success?

Having money is good, but did you know that money causes more problems in families and between people than almost anything else? The strange thing is that a

lot of people don't sit down and really talk about money until it's already a big problem.

If you and your family suddenly became very rich, how do you think your life would change? What would stay the same?

In today's hectic, fast-paced times, some people are consumed by money: "I need to make more money. I need to buy more things. I need to work harder to get even more money. There's no time to sleep, eat, or smell the roses. I need money to pay for everything I just bought and am about to buy." Benjamin Franklin, one of America's founding fathers, said, "Moderation in all things." What do you think that means?

Imagine you are at a big buffet. Food is piled up in trays all down the long table. Rather than pig out, the best thing to do is to take a little bit of several things you think you will like. Eat slowly, and enjoy the tastes. If you can resist going back for more, good for you. If chicken wings or cheese sticks are among the yummy delights, it may be very hard to pass up a second helping, but that's moderation.

A PERSON WITH MONEY SMARTS . . .

* doesn't keep giving in to the little voice in his or her head that screams, "I want it now!"

* is happy with what he or she has.

* is not unhappy because of what he or she doesn't have.

* knows how to make money work for him or her.

* is usually careful and precise with money.

* is not wasteful.

Here are eight ideas to help you jump-start your money smarts:

1. **Make a plan.**

You've looked into your future—or the future you'd like to have. How will you get there? Keep a record of money goals to reach by the time you turn twelve, or fifteen, eighteen, or twenty-one. Your goals will probably change as you grow. You also need to make another list—of what you can do now to help you reach your goals. Be as specific as possible.

2. **Find a money mentor, someone you trust who can give you advice about handling money.**

Ask this family member or family friend who wants the best for you to help you put together a money plan and set realistic goals.

3. **Use allowance as a dress rehearsal for the real thing— a paycheck.**

Each week, you have a certain amount of money. Make up a budget. Allot some of your cash for snacks, clothes, fun with friends, and savings. If you don't get an allowance, pretend that you do, and imagine how you would budget your cash. The more practice you have making money decisions, the smarter your money choices will be.

4. Know your money style. Are you a spender or a saver?

For some people, saving is almost second nature. For others, spending comes way too easily. And people who know what it's like not to have much money may develop strange money habits. They may hoard all their money for fear of losing it. If you are a saver by nature, it doesn't mean you're a better person than someone who loves to spend. It does mean that you are off to a good start toward managing your money. If, by nature, you seem to be more of a spender, arm yourself with ideas and information to help yourself save your money. (This book should help the cause.)

5. Learn from your mistakes.

Got ripped off? Waited too long for the price to drop on those jeans, and now they're not in the store? You will no doubt make lots of smart and not-so-smart choices. Many of these choices will stick with you for life and will become your money stories. Share them with your friends. Learn from them by talking about what you could have done to change each outcome so that it would have been a smart money move.

6. Keep a money journal of your ideas about money and the things you buy or want to buy. Start with responses to questions like these:

What was the last thing you bought with your own money? How did it make you feel? If you could buy anything right now, what would it be? What would you like to buy for someone else? How does spending money make you feel?

7. Create a money club with friends. Have each member contribute a few bucks each month.

What can you buy? What can you save for? How can you invest that money to make more money? (See pages 71–84 for some ideas.) How about starting a business with your friends? (See pages 44–48 for some ideas.)

8. **Pay attention to the economy. Get in the habit of reading the financial pages in the newspaper or on a news website.**

   Learn about companies that may be worthy of investing in. Think about how the economy affects your life.

FIVE MONEY GOALS

Set clear goals when it comes to money. If something changes—maybe you no longer want to save up to see turtles—revise your goals.

What I Want

1. To increase my college fund.
2. To own the latest technology gadgets and toys, like a watch that's also a phone.
3. To own designer clothes.
4. To be able to donate money to a cause that's important to me (wildlife conservation).
5. ~~To save up for a scooter.~~ To save up for a car.

What I Need to Do

1. Save, study hard, and apply for scholarships.
2. Set aside money for big purchases each week.
3. Learn to be a smarter shopper.
4. Collect spare change in a fund; volunteer for fund-raising activities.
5. Develop hobbies that can be turned into moneymakers.

3
Making It

epending on how old you are, your income will probably be more or less limited. Still, there will be times when you'll have cash in your pocket and a chance to make more. For most kids, the big source of income is allowance.

ALLOWANCE—THE BIG *A*

Allowance is money that some kids get regularly from their parents or a guardian. The idea is to give them practice spending, saving, sharing, and keeping track of their own money. The money you get in allowance is supposed to make you think about how much things cost so you will learn to make smart money decisions. It also teaches you to appreciate the items that you are able to buy.

If you get an allowance, you have a chance to show how responsible you are with money. If your parents have said no to an allowance, try to respect that. Remember that there are

ways to earn money, as you'll see in the next section. And, when you start showing you are money smart, your parents may notice and reconsider the allowance.

Chores or not

Lots of families link allowance to chores. Kids may get an agreed-upon amount of money each week as payment for setting the table, emptying the dishwasher, making the beds, or taking out the trash. If you don't do your chores, you may not get your allowance.

Some families believe that allowance should not be tied to chores. They believe that household chores are what you do as a member of the family, and you shouldn't be paid for something you are expected to do. The theory is that the grown-ups don't get an allowance for making dinner or doing the laundry, so why should the kids?

But many families agree that some chores, those that take up more time or effort, such as painting the fence or cleaning out the attic, may call for a few extra bucks.

Some money experts believe that allowance should be distributed on a regular basis, on a set day, at a specific time, like Fridays at 4:00 p.m. After all, in the real world, people get paid at a set time. Allowance is much easier to keep track of that way, too.

It's worth noting that when you spend your own money, you may be less willing to part with the big dollars. If it's coming from your pocket, you may decide to buy the cheaper jacket so that you'll also be able to save a little cash. Or you may find yourself taking better care of the stuff you buy. If you can keep something looking new, you won't have to replace it. That means more cash in your pocket.

ALLOWANCE DOS AND DON'TS

Dos

* Do be reasonable. If your parents tell you that they can't afford allowance, respect that and understand that they have their own budgetary constraints. What other ways can you earn some money? (See pages 44–48.)

* Do create the ground rules with your parents before money is exchanged. Will allowance cover school lunches? Friends' birthday presents? Charitable donations?

* Do establish with your parents a set time each week to get your allowance. (Tell them that's the way it is in the real world!)

* Do ask your parents for advice about how to budget your money.

* Do learn from your allowance mistakes.

* Do keep a record of where your money goes.

* Do plan your purchases before you go shopping.

* Do keep your allowance in a safe place.

* Do remember to include sales tax when planning out your purchases.

Don'ts

* Don't spend every penny of your allowance. Leave at least a little for savings and sharing.

* Don't fret if you blow some of your money; make a pact with yourself that next week you'll be smarter with it.

* Don't buy anything major with your money until you've thought about it carefully.

* Don't be upset if your friends get more allowance than you; accept the challenge of trying to stretch your cash.

* Don't ask for a raise in allowance if you do a good job at school. Ask for a hug instead.

How much allowance should you get?

Some money experts suggest a weekly allowance of a dollar for each year of your life. So, if you're nine, you would get nine dollars a week. Others believe it should depend on these factors:

* What your parents can afford. The amount has to meet their budget.

* How much other kids your age with similar needs are getting.

* Where you live. In places like New York or California, things usually cost more than they do in Iowa or Montana.

Managing allowance

For most kids, allowance is not adjustable. You get the same amount every week, even if that week happens to include a holiday. So it is up to you to plan ahead and save for special items or occasions throughout the year.

Expect to make a few mistakes with your money. You may find that one week, you've spent most of your allowance by Wednesday. When that happens, try to save more the following week. Don't be too hard on yourself if you've spent too much; remember, we learn from our mistakes.

PLAN IT OUT FIRST. Know how much you plan to save, spend, and share in the coming week. Planning ahead may eliminate unplanned spending.

DON'T LOSE IT. Keep it in a safe place. Carrying cash around with you all the time is not smart. If your money is not in your pocket, you won't spend it.

When it's time to ask for a raise

Want a raise in your allowance? Here are some things to think about before you ask your parents for more allowance. Keep in mind that if you can do this well, it will serve as excellent practice for asking for a pay raise once you have a job.

1. Prove to your parents that you are being responsible about money. Talk about how you have cut down on cell phone data usage (a big cost to many parents), have saved electricity costs by shutting off lights, or have been limiting yourself to one treat from the cafeteria per week.

2. Offer to take on new responsibilities, either in return for the raise or just because you are eager to help out.

3. Show your parents your weekly or monthly budget. Be organized. Explain how you've managed to increase savings and decrease spending.
4. Remain calm. A bad reaction from you can make things worse.

Save it!

Here are eleven quick-and-easy ways to save cash!

1. Make, don't buy, costumes. Use old clothes and items from around the house to craft something original.
2. Swap clothing with friends.
3. Check out eBay and secondhand stores. There's a lot of cheap vintage stuff out there.
4. Swap books with your friends or use the library.
5. When going out to eat, order water instead of soda; it's free—and also good for you!
6. Attend free concerts in the park and other free community events.
7. Clip coupons for personal items you use, such as hair gel, body lotion, or nail polish.
8. Get together with friends to have a community garage sale. Combine your baby furniture, toys, clothes, and books.
9. Don't browse stores with wads of cash in your pockets.
10. Make your own stationery and your own holiday and birthday cards.
11. Limit buying snacks when you are at the park or the mall.

SMART MONEY TIPS

Instant Saving

Ask your parents to give you five $1 bills instead of a $5 bill, or ten $1 bills instead of a $10 bill. That way, you can immediately set aside a few dollars for saving and sharing.

Perfect Records

Keep a shoe box to hold sales receipts from stuff that you buy with your allowance. Store the box where you can find it easily. If you need to return something, you'll have your receipt and a record of your purchase.

CAN WORK "WORK" FOR YOU?

If you ask a teacher or your parents how to make a lot of money, they might tell you that one day in the not-so-distant future, you will—drumroll, please—join the workforce.

Dentist, doctor, nurse, web developer, accountant, physical therapist, math teacher.

These are jobs that offer a smart mix of good money, job security, and work-life balance, according to a 2015 study in *US News and World Report*.

Get an edge on the work world by getting a job now. What will you gain? You'll learn to deal with all sorts of people. You'll get a heads-up about managing money, and you could have a nice pile of cold, hard cash before you hit your teen years. (It's never too early to start saving for a car or college!)

Whether it's fixing computers, taking photos, mowing lawns, babysitting, recycling cans, pet-sitting, or doing odd jobs for neighbors, young people today can definitely make a buck. And if you are savvy, you can become a successful entrepreneur (pronounced ahn-treh-preh-NURR)—meaning you run your own business. So, if you're too young for a work permit, or if you don't yet have the means to take on a job waiting tables or doling out ice cream, don't worry: there's a lot out there that you can do.

Are you ready for a job?

How do you know when it's time to get a job? Ask yourself the questions below and select the answer that best describes how you feel.

1. **Do you find yourself with too much time on your hands?**
   a. Yep. **b.** Nope, I like to watch the dust form on my windowsill.

2. **Do you wish you could meet new people?**
   a. Yep. **b.** Nope, I just chill with my phone.

3. **Do you want to learn something, other than the words to your favorite commercials?**
   a. Yep. **b.** Nope, silly jingles are my life.

4. **Would you like to earn some pocket money?**
   a. Yep. **b.** Nope, my parents have my back.

5. **Do you spend your allowance like it's going out of style?**
   a. Yep. **b.** Nope, I spend it before I get it.

6. **Are you tired of asking—make that begging—for money?**
   a. Yep. **b.** Nope, I have no problem asking over and over!

Your score

If you answered "yep" to three or more questions, it's time to get a job!

Be your own boss

Make some money by starting and managing a business. A successful entrepreneur is:

imaginative	**It takes imagination to come up with a bold idea.**
creative	**It takes a ton of creative juice to design something fresh and new.**
energetic	**You need energy to start up a new business. It may take twenty-five tries.**
determined	**You won't give up. There is a way to work it out, and you'll find it.**
organized	**You keep excellent records and can stick to your budget.**

Find a business here to match your skills. Try one or two or three.

Love tots?

If you have a way with little kids, be a babysitter. Parents are often willing to pay well for a friendly and reliable babysitter. If you're too young to babysit on your own, be a parent's helper—you can feed, play with, or read to a toddler while a parent does work around the house or cares for another child. By the time you're old enough to babysit on your own, you'll have some good contacts.

Tip: Enhance your skills by taking a babysitting class at your local YMCA or Red Cross chapter. You may learn first aid and safety tips that will come in handy when you're on the job.

Like to play with cars?

Team up with a few friends to provide a car-washing service. Remember, people who care about their cars need them washed at least once a month. Find out what a car wash goes for in your area and set your prices a little lower. If you do a good job, you'll have steady business all spring and summer.

Tip: When working with others, divide the work into various jobs. One person can greet the customer, another can wet and rinse the car, another can vacuum, another can dry the windows, and another can take the money and give a receipt. Take turns so that each person gets a chance to do each task.

Come to life in the company of animals?

Earn daily dollars by walking, grooming, or watching animals. Send out flyers and offer new customers a discount coupon. Give your pet business a zippy name, like Monkey Biz, Furry Friends, or Dog Days.

Tip: This is the kind of business that really takes off if customers trust and like you. Make your references available. Go the extra mile. Make a daily report that includes details about what the pet did that day and give it to the customer. If you are grooming a dog, be sure not to leave a wet mess and, for a special touch, tie a bright ribbon in the dog's fur.

Outdoors is where you want to be?

You can offer a complete line of lawn care services including mowing, weeding, trimming, and flower maintenance. Work with a small group of friends, make it a goal to get a new customer every week, and always leave the yard neat and tidy.

Tip: Type up your prices and let the customer know exactly what you expect to be paid before you start to work.

Chef in the making?

Go beyond the lemonade stand—how about an outdoor café? Offer herbal iced teas, soft drinks, and gourmet lemonade (lemonade poured over a cup of crushed ice). Maybe throw in some baked goods if you like sweets. Set your refreshments on a wagon or cart. Post a menu with prices. Get permission to set up at garage sales and other community events, or near a playground, tennis court, or pool. Good prices and the right location are key.

Tip: Offer free samples to tempt customers, bring lots of coins to make change, and dress up your refreshment stand with a colorful paper tablecloth.

Handy with details?

Be on-hand help or a personal assistant for a day. You can offer to do anything from closet cleaning to shoe shining, to shopping, to repotting plants, to helping plan a party.

Tip: Make a list of all the services you can offer to give to your customers. Smile and take your work seriously.

Super tech savvy?

Use your computer and graphic design skills to create sensational mailers, personalized holiday cards, or family newsletters.

Tip: If you can type, design, and publish on the computer, present your customers with a folder of your samples. You can create signs, banners, personalized calendars, stationery, or offer a typing service. Charge by the page.

Good at arts and crafts?

Make your own picture frames, beaded jewelry, T-shirts, 3-D animal bookmarks (made from felt scraps and buttons), or sell personalized scrapbooks. Ask a parent or guardian if they can help you sell your pieces in an online marketplace, like Etsy.

Tip: When you present your design samples, have price lists and order forms handy. Take all your supply costs into account and the amount of profit you want to make per item before setting your prices.

Make 'em laugh?

Be the entertainment at birthday parties for toddlers. Wear a costume. Many popular characters come in kid-sized costumes. Invest in a face-painting kit. Make sure to have some favorite children's books on hand. If there's a lull in the party, you can share a favorite story.

Tip: When working with young children, have a bunch of ideas up your sleeve, clean up as you go, and always make sure that safety is your biggest concern.

Weathered a storm?

If you live in a snowy climate, cash in on it! Team up with a pal, invest in a few shovels, and clear driveways and sidewalks of snow. Lots of snow could mean lots of dough!

Tip: Make arrangements with your regular customers to shovel snow after every snowfall.

First things first

Before your business blasts off, always make sure that:

* You are safe. Make sure your parents know where you are at all times. Also make sure you are comfortable with the job you are doing, and that you have all the information you need to complete the task. Never sell door-to-door by yourself. Trust your instincts; if something doesn't feel right, don't do it.

* You've worked out exactly how much money you need to start up your business. Have a plan. Where is the money coming from to buy the supplies? How much money do you want to earn? Will you be able to make a profit?

* You learn as much as possible about the job you are doing. If you are taking care of dogs, you'd better know

about dogs. If you are going to do lawn work, you need to know how to weed and trim. If you are going to sell gourmet snacks, select several tried-and-true recipes that are easy to prepare.

❋ You like what you do. If you are miserable doing the job you've chosen, it's probably not the job for you. Find something that you enjoy doing and can do well.

❋ It fits your schedule. School comes before your business; so do basketball practice and violin lessons. Make sure to check your calendar and allow yourself plenty of time to complete your jobs.

❋ It stays your job, not someone else's. If the job you've set for yourself becomes too much for you, don't pass it off to Mom or Dad. That's just not right.

❋ You are fair with prices. When setting up prices for your goods, total up the cost of all your materials and add something for time and labor. You will want to cover all your expenses, plus make a little profit. If you are setting an hourly rate for a service, find out what other kids are charging for similar jobs.

❋ You act like a professional. Be on time, greet your customers with a smile, treat them well, and do your work responsibly.

❋ You make time for work and play. Ask a parent or grown-up for advice or help if you're getting overwhelmed.

❋ You put some profit back into the business. For example, if you've got a lawn care business, you could use some of the money you've made to buy a new gardening tool that would allow you to trim the hedges more quickly.

❋ You are serious about the job. Keep track of your hours and make a commitment to yourself to do the best job possible.

TEN WAYS TO INCREASE EARNING POWER

1. **READ THE NEWSPAPER.** If you know what's going on in the world, you'll be able to talk to people.

2. **PRACTICE THE ART OF CASUAL CONVERSATION.** Get in the habit of saying "hello" and "how are you" to the people in your path.

3. **ALWAYS PUT YOUR BEST FOOT FORWARD.** If you have an interview for a job, look neat and clean.

4. **BE AN EYE-CONTACT SORT OF A KID.** Always look people in the eye when you talk to them. This puts them at ease and lets them know you're sincere and trustworthy.

5. **NEGOTIATE.** If somebody offers you a job and the pay doesn't sound quite right to you, or the hours are long, don't just accept the deal. Try to get the best arrangement for yourself. After all, you're worth it.

6. **SELL YOURSELF.** Know your strong points. Know your weak points. Write them down. Are you good with a

scooter, a frying pan, or a calculator? Could you use more help in science and basketball? Be prepared to talk about your strong points. Learn to present your weak points in a positive way, or try to focus on weak points that you won't need in the job you're applying for. For example, "I'm working on improving my public speaking; I don't believe that's a big part of this job, but I think public speaking is a good skill to have, no matter what."

7. BE INTERESTING. Talk about your personal experiences and mention several things that you like to do for fun.

8. STAND TALL. Good posture is key.

9. WATCH YOUR BODY LANGUAGE. Keep your hands out of your pockets, and don't look bored or tired. Smiling is good.

10. KEEP YOUR SENSE OF HUMOR AT ALL TIMES. That helps to put others at ease and makes any awkward situation a lot easier to deal with.

FUTURE FORTUNE

Work. It may be a four-letter word, but that doesn't mean it can't be awesome. Whether it's a job you're taking on right now, or your future career, you should love what you do and get enjoyment out of it—in addition to money.

4

Using Your Money Smarts

*n*ow that you're getting an allowance, the money is all in your hands. And money is not always easy to hold on to. How can you manage your income and spending?

DID YOU SAY BUDGET?

A budget is a plan that helps you keep track of your money. It lets you know how much comes in (income) and where all that money goes (the candy store, the movies) so you can control your spending. With practice, making a budget and sticking to it will become easy. Soon you'll wish you had started before you frittered away all that cash! But there's no time like the present. And budgeting can be a fun and rewarding challenge, especially if you set yourself realistic money goals.

The first step in setting up a budget is to find out exactly where you are right now. You do this by making a list of your

Budget

Average weekly income:

Allowance	$15
Lunch money	$12
Odd jobs	$22
Total	$49

Next, list your weekly expenses.

Average weekly expenses:

School lunch	$10
Snacks	$6
Clothes/accessories	$12
Entertainment (games, movies, books, etc.)	$10
Drugstore and miscellaneous spending	$5
Total	$43

$49 – $43 = $6 for saving, sharing, investing

income (where your money comes from every week) and your expenses (where your money goes every week).

Balancing your budget means subtracting your expenses from your total income. If you get a negative number, you are spending too much. You are over budget! You need to get back on budget by either increasing your income or decreasing your expenses.

Now that you have figured out where your money is going, you can look for ways to cut back on spending. For example, do you really need to be spending an average of $10 each week on entertainment? Why not swap books and movies with friends? Could you bring your lunch from home at least two days a week for more savings?

The trick to budgeting is finding a formula that's right for you. Do you prefer budgeting on a weekly basis? Or would a monthly budget be better for you? Do you like to keep track of things on the computer or by hand? Do you carry around a small notebook, so you can easily jot down expenses? Do you save receipts and add up exact amounts, or round off expenses by to memory? Remember, saving money means learning to live on less than what you have. Sometimes you need to be inventive in coming up with new ways to trim the fat from your expenses.

Keep copies of your weekly budgets. Budgeting, like other important tasks, gets easier with time and experience.

THE FAMILY BUDGET

Does your family have a budget? What kind of expenses are involved in running a house? Ask your parents if they will show you their monthly budget. Can you offer any smart money-saving ideas? To save money, how about suggesting that your family buy some items, such as paper goods or dry cereal, in bulk?

MONEY JAMS

For every problem, there is usually a solution—maybe even several solutions! Here are some budgeting scenarios to rev up your problem-solving brain:

The problem

I like trendy stuff. I want whatever is new and hip. I know that I am wasting a lot of money because what's in now is never in a few months later. But I am still a sucker for the latest trendy looks.

A solution

Limit yourself to one trendy item every other month. Being fashionable can be expensive. If you really are a trendy person, be a trendsetter—sew cool fabric patches on your jeans, make awesome bags out of colored felt. Turn items you already own into fashion statements. That's called being trendy on a budget.

The problem

I have a close friend who always has cash. Every time we go somewhere and I am short on cash, he offers to pay for me. I don't think my parents would want me borrowing money from anyone, but I am too embarrassed to tell my friend that I can't afford his friendship. What should I do?

A solution

Some people who have a lot of money have no idea what it's like not to have a lot of money. That's why you have to let your situation be known. Come clean to your parents. Ask them if you can borrow the money to pay back your friend. Then, explain to your close friend that money is tight. Encourage your friend to spend time with you doing things that don't require huge gobs of cash—like hanging out in the park or taking a walk. You get the idea.

The problem

My best friend and I have the same birthday! We exchanged birthday gifts, but she spent $5 on my gift and I spent $20 on hers. Now we both feel awkward.

A solution

Don't let this birthday mishap strain your friendship. Laugh it off. Next year, set a dollar limit on the amount that you will spend for birthday presents or take each other out for pizza and ice cream.

The problem

I never buy anything without doing research. How much does the item cost? Where else can I buy it? Is there any way I can get it cheaper? It's a real challenge for me, but my friends make fun of me all the time. They think I am cheap and that I should just buy what I want without thinking about it.

A solution

Get your friends interested in comparison shopping by letting them know how much money you've saved from all your research. Offer to help them comparison shop with their next purchase. They'll thank you for it in the end because wasting money is not cool.

SPEND, SPEND, THEN SPEND MORE, PLEASE!

Welcome to the consumer culture. You know, you've got to get the best one, the deluxe model, the top of the line, and you've gotta have it now! It's great to be a consumer, but when you're buying, look for quality and try not to overspend.

Advertising is not what it appears

If you're like most kids, you've spent a lot of time watching TV. By now, you've probably absorbed some thirty thousand commercials. That's a lot of powerful messages about candy, cereal, fast-food treats, and toys. And, if you're like many kids, you may believe that crunchy candy can make you popular and happy, the doll will grant you instant friends, or the cereal will make you superstrong and smart. Think about the last time you bought something based on a promise from a TV commercial. Did the product live up to its promise?

Just because we see something advertised doesn't mean the product is really the best. It just means that some people paid a lot of money to get airtime for their product.

Advertisers are seeking you out. They want you to spend all your money on their products. And advertisements are not just on television. They are all over the Internet, on billboards, on the backs of cereal boxes, on the radio, and on those company logos on our clothes.

THE IGB TEST

Step One

Drop it. Let go of the item. Release it. Blink your eyes to erase the item from your vision. Then stick a mental picture of the item in the window of your imagination (in your head).

Step Two

Step away from the item. Change your perspective. Mentally flick the lights in the room. Walk around the store and come back. Is it still there? Do you still want it? Has something changed?

Step Three

Transform yourself into a person you know who has great money smarts. Is it a parent, a relative, a neighbor, or a friend? Now really look at your mental picture of the item as that person. Would that person want or need to buy that? Would that person think that buying that item would be a smart and savvy purchase?

Step Four

You must really want this thing because you've made it to step four! Now take out your mental image and talk to it. Tell it what you're expecting from it. Are you hoping to look cool because of it? Or seem a little smarter with it? Tell it what you want from it. Now, when you speak to it, does it talk back to you? If it does, if it really talks to you, then go buy it already!

Immediate gratification blaster

Try to resist the fancy computer, phone, or watch. The drone. Those jeans. The beaded necklace you absolutely have to own. The sneakers. (That's your third pair this year!) The new skateboard. All things you want. You may even think you need them. And maybe you do. And maybe you don't. You'll never know until you get with the Immediate Gratification Blaster program.

Immediate gratification—the need to have it now—is at the heart of an overspender's problem. An overspender might see something and not take the time to think about the purchase. Your inner voice tells you, "I need it now!"

Next time you find yourself face-to-face with the hottest fashion accessory since the temporary tattoo, or yearning to bite into a fancy wrap or sandwich that costs three times the price of a sandwich that you can make at home, give it the IGB test.

TIME TO SHOP

Imagine you are in your favorite clothing store. You are shopping for fall clothes for school, but a big sale sign catches your attention. It turns out all summer pants, shorts, and T-shirts are 75 percent off the regular price! That's a lot of savings. What will you do with your money? Spend it on fall clothes like you planned? Or do you take the opportunity to save money by buying items you know you will be needing, even if not for two or three seasons? It may be hard to think of buying summer clothes when the leaves are turning and Halloween is just around the corner. But if you're a really thrifty shopper, you'll think ahead. End-of-season sales are a good time to stock up.

Buying things out of season to give as gifts can be a great money-saving idea. And nobody but you has to know when you actually bought the stuff.

Impulse buying

Many purchases we make are unplanned. In some grocery stores, customers may be tempted with free samples of yummy, freshly made goods—apple cider, blueberry pie, and other gourmet treats. Shoppers who planned to buy just milk, eggs, and butter may fill their carts with dozens of other unplanned but delicious items. Impulse buying is not a bad thing unless it gets out of control.

Where to buy

Shopping today can mean a trip to a huge mall or a visit to a specialty or outlet store. Or it can mean sitting in your living room and using your computer. There are so many shopping alternatives.

Department and chain stores are great for buying a variety of things and usually have good sales. You may be able to find more original items of clothing or jewelry at specialty stores, which can be small and which are generally locally owned. And vintage shops are proof that some things truly are better the second time around.

Online shopping lets you buy everything from fine chocolate to daffodils to cool sneakers for extra-wide feet. With a few clicks of your mouse or taps on your screen, you can buy almost everything. But remember a few important things when you're shopping online:

* have a parent or an adult make sure that you are on a secure site.

* review the site's privacy statement before you purchase anything.

* print out the receipt and confirmation. This will serve as a record in case you have a problem with your order.

Be a smart consumer. Comparison shop. Judge different brands of products against each other. Talk to friends and relatives before you buy. Find out what brands they are most satisfied with. Research the product. Go to several different stores before making the purchase. Use coupons to save money on food and other items.

Make sure to check out the store's return policy so you can take back that new jacket you *had* to have if you decide next week that you don't like it anymore. If you can't return something, you could try to see if you can get money for it, and some of your other gently used clothes, at a thrift store or through an online service like Thredup (https://www.thredup.com).

5

Growing It

There's a real sense of accomplishment when you set a money goal and reach it. You feel independent and smart when you can buy something on your own, with money that you have saved up. It's kind of the same way you feel when you exercise, eat right, write a story or poem, or do something that you know is right and good for your mind and body.

TRY THIS

For the next two months, drop any spare change that you find in your pockets at the end of the day into a glass jar. Watch it grow. At the end of the two months, count the change. Then do something special with it—donate it to a good cause, put it in the bank, or set it aside for holiday gifts. That's money you probably forgot you had!

BANK ON IT!

Saving money means you'll have it if you need it for something you didn't plan for—if your bike needs repairs, or you lose your eyeglasses and need new ones. And then there are those things that you need or want but are expensive enough to have to save for—a watch that's also a computer, a new bedroom set, a car. The best way to be sure you have money for such things is by saving your money in the bank.

Earning interest

Ava saves her babysitting money in an old shoe box. She likes to keep a close eye on it. Every once in a while she likes to give the box a shake. But how could Ava make her money grow? By depositing it in the bank in a savings account, where it would earn interest.

How does interest work? Suppose you put $100 in the bank and the bank agrees to pay you 5 percent interest each year. That means that the bank will pay you 5 cents on every dollar each year. After the first year, you will have earned $5 in interest.

When your money is in the bank, it's safe. The bank has fireproof steel vaults that can be opened only by bank staff under tight security regulations. When you deposit your money in a bank account, the bank lends the

money out to someone else at a higher rate of interest than the bank is paying you. That's how the bank makes money. The bank pays you interest. That's how you make money. You can see the amount of money you get in interest when you get a bank statement. The money doesn't just sit there—it grows!

What if you cut out the middleman, the bank, and simply loaned your money to a friend and charged interest? How does that sound? Aha, but forget the interest, what if your friend doesn't even pay you back? You'd be out everything, even the friend. Sometimes borrowing and lending money sounds like a good idea, but it's always safer to do it officially, from a bank.

In the bank, the more money you have in a savings account, the more interest you earn. Many banks offer compound interest. That's better than just regular interest because you earn interest not only on your savings, but also on the interest you make on your savings. It gives you interest on your interest. Not bad!

Banks also offer special accounts called "certificates of deposit," or CDs. These bank CDs pay higher interest rates the longer you leave the money in the account—but if you need to take it out sooner, you will be charged a penalty fee. Bank CDs can be used toward your college education.

So check out the banks in your area. See what they offer. Here are some questions to ask while shopping for the right bank:

* How much interest will I earn on my savings?

* Can I do my banking online at no extra cost?

- ✳ Is my money insured (in case of fire, flood, or robbery)?

- ✳ Do I need to keep a minimum amount of money in the account?

- ✳ Will I be charged a monthly fee if I don't keep a minimum balance?

- ✳ Does a free ATM card come with this account?

Check for checking

Having a checking account means your money is safe. Checkbooks can be replaced if they are lost or stolen (but you do need to tell the bank about such a loss in writing as soon as you discover it). Cash cannot be replaced. It is just gone—and that's not a good feeling!

If you qualify as a checking account customer (banks sometimes have age restrictions), you receive a statement every month. The statement lists all the checks that you have written that have cleared the bank (which means they have been paid), each deposit you made, and charges for the bank's services. One drawback is that checking accounts don't pay as much interest as savings accounts. There are often other fees when you use checks, so if you just want to save money— not spend it—a savings account is the way to go.

Do you ATM?

ATM stands for automated teller machine, and ATM cards let you access money from your account via an ATM. This is so helpful when you need money on weekends, on holidays, or in the evenings, when banks are closed. If you are old enough, you can get an ATM card when you open a savings account. To use it, you will have to pick a personal identification number (called a PIN). This four-number code will be the code you enter into the ATM machine each time you use your card. This prevents someone else from using your card if it is lost or stolen. You will need to remember your PIN or keep it in a safe place—but not with the card!

ATM cards are not always the cheapest way to get to your money. Watch out for annual fees that every ATM cardholder must pay. Also, you might have to pay a fee each time you use your ATM card—if you use an ATM not connected to your bank. So before you whip that card out, consider the fees you'll be paying. Should your card get stolen or lost, call the bank right away. And remember: never, ever give your PIN to anyone!

Personal banking

Be organized when keeping track of your money. Keep all your financial records in order, so you can find things if you need to. Put copies of bank deposits and sales receipts for things you've bought—in case you need to return them—in files or labeled shoe boxes. Keep track of any payments made on large items and smaller loans that you have repaid—it's a good start on your credit history.

According to *US News and World Report*, if you bank at an online-only bank, you will be offered higher interest rates. Many of them do not have ATM fees or monthly fees. Online banking is considered safe if you follow certain precautions. Security experts recommend that you visit your banks through a bookmark that you create in your browser, or by typing your bank's URL directly into the address bar of your browser. Security experts advise not to log into an account from someone else's computer. Also, don't send your username, password or PIN, account info, or credit card information over e-mail. Print out bank statements so that you can refer back to them easily.

BEST PLACES
TO KEEP YOUR MONEY

Ready for a little quiz? In the following situations, which place—
a) a bank, b) a piggy bank, c) your wallet—is the best place to keep
your money?

1. When you are going to a store where the jacket you want is 50 percent off.

2. When all you can manage to save from your allowance each week is small change.

3. When you are looking for a special birthday gift.

4. When you are saving a part of your allowance for something that costs a lot.

5. When you are meeting someone you owe money to.

6. When your piggy bank is full.

7. When your allowance money just goes through your hands like water.

8. When you are treating a friend to the movies.

9. When you empty your pockets at night.

10. When you win $100 in an essay contest.

Answers:

1. c 2. b 3. c 4. a 5. c 6. a 7. a 8. c 9. b 10. a

Your assets

An adult may have a house, stocks and bonds, antiques, a car, and a vacation house. Those are his or her assets—all the things that the person owns, which add up to a certain amount of money.

What are your assets? They may include things given to you from relatives, such as an emerald ring or an antique doll. Your assets may include collectibles, such as coins, stamps, antiques, and jewelry. For some collectors, the items that they like increase in value. Sometimes, rather than sell such collections, older family members pass individual pieces on to young people who they think might enjoy or appreciate them.

Some valuable items sometimes find their way into thrift stores, flea markets, and garage sales and can be picked up for little money. But that doesn't mean you should run out and buy everything you see there.

INVESTING 101

Investing means putting your money to work in the hope that it will make you more money. The sooner you start investing your money, the more time it will have to grow. The more time your money has to grow, the better off you'll be.

There are many ways to invest money. The most common ways are in a savings bank where your money will earn interest, and in bonds, stocks, and mutual funds. We already know that banks pay us interest for keeping our money in a savings account, but how do bonds, stocks, and mutual funds work?

Bonds

Bonds are loans to companies or governments. The company or government promises to pay you back by a certain date and also gives you interest on your money—your loan. Many people give bonds as gifts to newborn babies or as birthday presents to kids. By buying the bonds, they feel they are lending money to help the country grow, and the bond appreciates (which means it is worth more) as the child grows up. The dollar amount that the person pays for the bond is called the principal. The amount of interest that the bond pays is usually determined by the strength of the government or company to pay back the principal plus the interest rate promised. United States government and savings bonds are considered very safe, but bonds from newly formed companies or troubled countries may be considered much more risky.

A typical bond purchase might be a bond with a value of $1,000 and a coupon of 8 percent maturity over the next ten years. What that means is, for the next ten years, you will receive $80 worth on interest each year. After ten years, you will get your $1,000 back. Bonds can be bought and sold easily online. You can buy them from http://treasurydirect.gov—a cool website where you can also play money-related games.

Stocks

A stock is a small piece, or share, of a company. People who own stocks are called shareholders. If you buy stock in a company and want your money back, you have to sell your stock. If you do sell your stock and the price is higher than when you bought it, you make money, and it could be a lot. But if the price of the stock is lower than when you bought it, you will lose money if you sell it. Stock prices go up and down all the time. There are thousands of stocks to choose from—and investors will usually diversify. That means they will buy a range of stocks that vary in size, style, and industry, or sector.

People who buy shares of a company do so for two reasons: dividends and value.

DIVIDENDS—As the company makes money, some of that money is paid out in dividends. Dividends are a portion of the company's earnings that get paid out to shareholders based on how much stock each person owns. The more shares you own, the more money you make.

VALUE—When a company grows, the value of the stock increases. The more valuable the company becomes, the higher the stock price goes.

Mutual funds

Mutual funds are lots of different stocks or bonds grouped together. When you buy shares in a mutual fund, you and many others own a very small part of the whole fund collection. A fund manager decides which stocks, bonds, and other investments to buy with the money collected from the investors. By investing in a mutual fund, you can own stocks in several different sectors— technology, medicine, international companies, or companies that protect the environment.

FINANCIAL CRISIS

Everyone talks about the financial crisis that happened in 2008. Here is a simple explanation for a very complicated issue.

Back in the 1990s, Americans wanted to buy bigger homes. People buy homes by borrowing money from banks. This is what is called a mortgage. The banks make a profit by loaning the money to the homebuyer and charging them a lot more money for the loan than the cost of the home. But many of the people who were given loans to buy homes were never going to be able to afford to pay back the loans. Homeowners often took the loans because they were given special incentives to buy homes. The bank may have offered them low monthly payments for two years. But at the end of two years, when the payments increased, many of the homeowners could not afford them.

After a while, banks lost a lot of money. Housing prices gradually dropped because no one could afford to buy homes without the help of the banks. Investors lost a lot of the money that they had put into the banks. This created major problems for the economy as a whole. But the government is working now to find ways to help banks, investors, and homeowners get back on their feet.

Six things to know about investing

If you're thinking of investing your money:

1. You will have to ask a parent or guardian to make your investments for you because you are a minor. In order to buy stock, you must be at least eighteen years old. You will need to open an account with a stockbroker, who will do the buying and selling for you. Accounts are opened in person, by mail, by phone, or on the Internet.

2. Your goal as an investor is to build an increasingly larger and more profitable portfolio, a collection of investments.

3. There are all kinds of investments with all kinds of risk. Some investments are very high risk. That means you may make a lot of money, but you also may lose a lot of money. Other investments are considered low risk or almost no risk. How you invest your money depends on your personality, your appetite for adventure, and what is happening in your life.

4. Ask questions about the investment you're considering: What if I end up with less money than I started with? How soon can I get my money if I need it? How can I find out more about the particular investment?

5. Know the risks involved and try to match your personality and situation to the right level of investment risk. If you like life in the fast lane, and you can afford to lose the money, go for it. But if you worry about losing your money, do something more

conservative. Of course, less risk may mean less profit on your money.

6. Don't put all your eggs in one basket. That means you should try to diversify; put money into several different kinds of investments, not in just one. That way, if you take a loss on something, chances are, you'll make a profit on something else.

What kind of investor will you be?

Are you a high-risk, medium-risk, or low-risk person? Do you enjoy taking big chances, or do you run from risks? If there's a 50 percent chance of rain in the forecast, do you take your umbrella and rain gear, or do you risk it? Find out about your risk level with this quiz. Which of the responses below best reflect your personality?

1. You have been selected to study abroad for a year. It's a great opportunity to learn, meet new people, and see the sights. You . . .

a. are packed and set to go.

b. are considering the trip, but you have a few second thoughts, like what will you do when you're homesick?

c. could never be away from your family for so long.

2. A new restaurant has just opened in your town, and everyone is raving about the exotic daily specials. Today's special is poached ostrich with sun-dried tomatoes and plum sauce. You . . .

a. go for it. Bon appétit!

b. are not quite willing to order the ostrich, but you agree to taste your friend's.

c. stick with something you know you like—the burger.

3. You and your family have just won a free trip to a gorgeous island near Hawaii. Only catch is, there's a one in six hundred chance that a giant volcano will erupt on that island while you are there. You . . .

a. go for it. Chances are, you'll be safe and sound.

b. go, but you make sure to take precautions and keep your head up for volcanic activity.

c. plead with your parents to make new vacation plans.

4. You're at a brand-new, state-of-the-art amusement park. The Rocking Rolling Coaster promises the ride of your life. You . . .

a. are first in line.

b. wait until your friends go on it to give you a report.

c. make a mad dash for the carousel.

5. As a contestant on the latest TV game show, you've just won $1,000. Now you have to decide whether to keep the money and stop the game, or trade the money in for what's behind the curtain. The prize could be a new computer, a check for $50,000, or a can of cat food. You . . .

a. go for the curtain.

b. ask for the input of the audience because you can't make up your mind.

c. keep the $1,000 and call yourself a big winner.

Your score

For each **a** response, give yourself 3 points. For each **b** response, give yourself 2 points. For each **c** response, give yourself 1 point.

Add up your score.

12–15 points ✳
Risky Frisky

Did someone say "bungee jumping"? Is "go for it" your motto? Risk takers love thrills and adventure. As far as investing goes, risk takers are aggressive, jumping in where other investors fear to tread. You could make a lot of dough . . . or lose a lot. But that's fine with you; you love living dangerously.

8–11 points ✳
Middle of the Road

Every once in a while, taking a big chance—tasting something exotic, seeing a blood-tingling horror flick, riding a huge wave—may appeal to you. But mostly, you seek comfort with a medium amount of risk. That's what you tend to look for in your investments, too—you make a steady but not huge amount from a careful investment, and then once in a while you may gain or lose a lot when you take a big risk.

5–7 points ✳
Caution on the Sidelines

Your idea of taking a risk might be buying a raffle ticket. You like to know what's going to happen next. You don't like the idea of making a mistake. That makes you a conservative investor. You are looking for a sure bet. You might not make a ton of money immediately, but it will build over time—and you won't lose a ton of money, either.

The stock market

Think of a street market or country fair, where people come with products to sell and others come wanting to buy. If a product is useful, there will be many people interested in buying it. This will raise the price of that product. On the other hand, if a product does not work well, people will not be too anxious to buy it and, after a while, the price of that product will go down. That, in essence, is what the stock market is. It is a meeting place, called an exchange, where buyers and sellers come together. Some will buy and some will sell.

In order for shares of stock to be traded, meaning bought and sold, there must be a buyer and a seller. But they don't talk face-to-face. Stockbrokers arrange the trade. The broker for the buyer says how much the buyer is willing to pay for each share of the stock. The broker for the seller says how much the seller wants to receive. If the two brokers can agree on a price, the trade is made. Essentially, if you want to invest in the stock market, you aim to buy low and sell high.

There are more than 140 exchanges all over the world. For example, there are stock markets in London, Paris, Hong Kong, and Tokyo. There are markets where only gold and precious metals are bought and sold. There are other markets that specialize in oil and gas, in rice and wheat, and in meat and soybeans.

Where the trades are made

The New York Stock Exchange (NYSE), the largest organized stock exchange in the United States, started out as nothing more than a dirt path in front of a church in east New York two hundred years ago. At that time, there was no paper money changing hands and there were no stocks to buy. Silver, coming in on ships, was traded daily. In 1792, twenty-four men signed an agreement that established the NYSE.

Wall Street, the financial district of New York, boomed in the early 1900s with the Industrial Revolution. Suddenly, the NYSE was not the only way to buy stocks. Some stocks that didn't make it onto the NYSE were traded outside on the curb. Formal rules and regulations transformed this open, outdoor "curb market" into an organized exchange, and it moved indoors. In 1953, the New York Curb Exchange was renamed the American Stock Exchange (AMEX). The AMEX is the nation's second-largest equities market, and it attracts and lists smaller companies than the NYSE.

The National Association of Securities Dealers Automatic Quotation System (NASDAQ) is different from the other two exchanges because it has no physical location. All trading is done by computer.

The Dow Jones Industrial Average (DJIA) is a daily measure of the overall performance of the stock market. The DJIA is the daily average of thirty stocks. If the average value of those stocks goes down, we say the stock has decreased. If the average value of those stocks goes up, we say the stock has increased.

Blue-chip stocks are the largest, most consistently profitable companies. The term comes from gambling. In poker, where plastic chips are used instead of money, the most valuable chips are the blue ones. Some historical blue-chip stocks are General Electric, IBM, and General Motors. Today, blue-chips stocks might include McDonald's, Walmart, and Microsoft.

Two animals represent the movement of stocks up or down. A bull market is an increase in stock prices, while a bear market is a decrease in stock prices.

Learning about investing

Want to learn more about investing? Here's what you can do.

* Create an investment club and keep track of stocks. Use play money or have a parent sponsor you by making the investments for you.

* Watch the stock market closely. You and a friend can each select a stock to track. At the end of the month, determine who made the best investment. Who would have lost money? Make a graph to see how the stock climbed or fell.

* Let friends and family know that you are learning about investing and wouldn't mind bonds, stocks, and mutual funds as gifts instead of cash or clothes.

* Start comparing stocks. Find a blue-chip company to learn more about. Ask an adult to help you request an annual report. What are the strengths and weaknesses of the company?

* Learn more about the stock market and the different companies represented in it from newspapers, television shows, and company reports.

THE STOCK REPORT

To find the current value of a stock and other information about it, flip or click to the business section of a newspaper. Look for a listing of stocks in columns that looks something like this:

1	2	3	4	5	6	7	8
52-week							
High Low	Symbol	Name	Div.	EPS	P/E	Last	Chg.
38 23	MM	Marlee's Muffins	.10	.07	12	27.17	+.22

1. The highest and lowest prices of the stock over the past fifty-two weeks. This tells you how much the value of the stock has changed in a year—$38 was the high price per share and $23 was the low price.

2. Sometimes the name, logo, or symbol for the company (usually one to three letters) is given. For example, here "MM" stands for Marlee's Muffins. This is also called the ticker symbol.

3. The company name—it may be shortened but should be recognizable.

4. The dividend that some companies pay to shareholders. The dividend amount is the portion of the profits paid out per share.

5. The earnings per share. A company's EPS is the amount of profit the company made over the past year divided by the number of shares.

6. The price-to-earnings ratio. The P/E ratio comes from dividing the current price of a share by the earnings per share. A high P/E means investors are willing to pay top dollar for the stock.

7. The latest price of the stock, based on the last stock market session.

8. The amount of price change during the last session. In the case of MM, the company gained 22 cents. This may not seem like much, but if someone owns 100 shares of stock, they've just made $22.

Nowadays, it's a snap to get stock quotes off the Internet. The information is constantly being updated. Check out sites like www.marketwatch.com or any major newspaper's website. Enter the ticker symbol in the quote box.

CALLING ALL COLLECTORS

Stamps. Coins. Seashells. Dolls. Stickers. What do these things have in common? They are all items that people collect. Whether it's perfume atomizers, postcards, autographs, stuffed animals, puppets, trading cards, or sports memorabilia, collecting can be a lifelong passion—and a safe way to invest your money.

6

Be in Control

redit cards let you buy things without having the cash in hand. But we pay for this plastic luxury. Some people who may be light on money smarts may pay greatly. Many fall victim to the dangers of out-of-control credit card spending. Don't worry—if you're smart about credit cards, you won't be one of them.

TO YOUR CREDIT

"Attention, young people!" Finance companies will be tracking you down. They may soon be sending you mail, promising you low interest rates, gift incentives, free bonuses, and more to get you to order their credit card. Actually, college-age kids are the number one target for credit card companies looking for fresh customers. Learn all you can now about how credit cards work so that, by the time you are in college, you will know how to use a credit card responsibly.

Some finance companies offer tweens and teens their own credit cards. Let's say you're going to boarding school, or you're taking a trip across the country for the summer. You'll definitely need some money. Rather than cash, a credit card may come in handy. Credit cards allow you to spend money you don't have, on loan from the company, and then pay it back in monthly installments with interest. But credit cards don't generally come with a user's guide. First-time users often don't see how much they have to pay in monthly interest fees in exchange for the convenience of buying on credit.

What's good about credit cards?

THEY ARE IDEAL WHEN YOU ARE IN A BIND. You never know when you will find yourself in a situation that requires money fast.

THEY ARE ACCEPTED ALL OVER THE WORLD. Whether you find yourself in Tahiti, Alaska, or Egypt, you can just whip out your card. And no need to worry about changing currency and searching out the right amount—the credit card company does all the calculating for you. If you are planning to travel, let your credit card company know in advance. If they see charges on your card coming out of Bangladesh (or anywhere else far from wherever you live), they won't question it.

THEY PROTECT YOU IN CASE OF THEFT. You don't have to worry about someone stealing your cash if you don't carry any. And what if your credit card is lost or stolen? Report it immediately and the card will be canceled. Then you will be issued a new one.

What's bad about credit cards?

ANNUAL FEES. For each credit card you own and use, you may be charged a fee.

INTEREST FEES. You're required to make only a minimum payment each month, but unless you pay off the full amount of the bill when you get it, the outstanding balance collects interest. Some credit card companies charge as much as 20 percent in interest.

YOU CAN START SPENDING MORE THAN YOU CAN ACTUALLY AFFORD. It sounds great to buy now, pay later, but that kind of spending can result in major credit card debt. This is a very hard concept for many people to grasp. If you have always been short on money but suddenly get a piece of plastic that can buy you the world, it's going to be hard to resist. What you need to know is that buying on credit can cost a lot of money— money that you didn't have in the first place.

Here's what you need to know

Congratulations, you have just received your first credit card! Read these facts and remember them each time you swipe it.

* Plastic money is not free money. Charge only what you know you can afford to pay back.

* Charges should be paid back as soon as possible. When bills aren't paid in full, the outstanding balance collects interest. You run the risk of having to pay charges that you cannot catch up on.

* If you lose your card, notify the card company immediately to avoid having to be responsible for charges that don't belong to you.

* If you move, remember to update your contact information promptly to avoid any late charges.

* Review your monthly statement carefully. Make sure you can identify all charges. It may not be likely, but credit card companies sometimes do make mistakes, and it's up to you to find them.

* Beware of credit card companies that offer big incentives for you to spend, spend, spend. Once you start abusing your credit card, it's very difficult to stop. Habits are hard to change.

* Think of your future. Credit problems stay with you. Binge out on credit cards now, and you may not be able to get a student loan, buy a car, or own a home. If a company isn't certain that you will pay back the loan, why should it loan you money?

* When you become a credit card holder, you have an opportunity to prove that you can pay your bills on time. Your information gets transferred to a credit card report. This report will help you later in life when an employer, landlord, or insurance company is trying to find out details about your credit profile.

IDENTITY CRISIS!

Olivia, an eighteen-year-old college student, was working on her laptop at a local café. After studying for a while, Olivia started to surf the net to do some shopping. What she didn't know was that a stranger was behind her doing something called "shoulder surfing." The stranger looking over Olivia's shoulder was busy stealing Olivia's personal information.

A week later, Olivia was reviewing her monthly bank statement when she noticed something was not right. There were $3,000 worth of charges to stores that Olivia had never even heard of! That's when she knew that she was a victim of identity theft. Identity theft is when a person uses your personal information without your permission. Doing this is fraud. It is illegal.

Unlike your fingerprints, which are unique to you, a person's credit card information, Social Security number, and health information can be stolen. Identity thieves will use this information to buy things, apply for new credit cards, take out loans, and make health-care claims. If you don't catch these charges, you may be the one to pay them!

It's a good thing Olivia was in the habit of reviewing her bank statement each month, or she might not have seen or questioned the fraudulent charges. Those charges could have kept on coming.

Olivia immediately contacted her credit card company and then the Federal Trade Commission (FTC) at 1-877-ID THEFT to report the crime.

Here is a list of ways you can protect yourself from identity theft:

* If your bank card or credit card is stolen or lost, report it immediately to your bank and the Federal Trade Commission.
* If possible, do not conduct online shopping transactions over a public Wi-Fi connection, like at a café. It's easier for people to hack public Wi-Fi networks and steal your information.
* If you do need to make purchases in public, be aware of people trying to look over your shoulder. When you enter your PIN or password at the ATM machine, make sure no one is standing too close to you.
* Keep watch of your mailbox. If you leave home for a few days, have a trusted friend hold your mail for you.
* Tear up or shred pieces of mail that contain personal information about you.
* Store your passwords in a secure place. Don't talk about them to friends. Change them every few months.
* Read your bank statement carefully every month. Look for unfamiliar charges.
* Review your credit reports often. Look for changes.

Identity theft is a serious problem. Every year, nine million Americans fall victim to some form of identity theft.

BEWARE OF PHISHING

What's phishing? Those phony e-mails that almost everyone gets. They are e-mails claiming to be from well-known companies asking for personal information from you in order to register you for something. If you get such an e-mail, do not respond—this is another way someone can get access to your personal information.

THE GOLD IN GIVING

People give money, time, or sometimes goods because they want to make the world a better place. What is more satisfying than knowing that a donation you made is improving someone's life?

How much you give depends on how you look at money and how much you can afford to give. Some people try to tithe, meaning give 10 percent of their earnings to a recognized charitable or cultural organization. If you like to read, you might give to a local organization that helps kids who are learning to read. If you like animals, you might give to a local shelter. But the choice is up to you. Everyone's financial situation is different.

Giving on a regular basis works well because it makes giving a habit—a part of your budget and a part of your life. You can choose to make a monthly, twice yearly, or yearly donation, or you may want to simply give loose change when you have it.

In addition to money, many organizations will appreciate your offer of a more personal helping hand.

Be a fund-raiser

If you don't have money to spare, you and your friends may want to host a fund-raising event for an organization you like. Try any of these fun fund-raising ideas:

Hold a bake sale

A group of friends, a supervising adult, and an afternoon in the kitchen can yield muffins, cookies, cakes, and pies that you can sell in the park, near a shopping mall, or in front of your local library. Let your customers know where the proceeds are going. Also, keep a big jar on hand for additional donations. As a nice thank-you, offer customers a recipe or two written on small index cards.

Have a car wash

Ask your parents and your friends' parents to donate old towels, rags, sponges, and buckets. Post signs about your car wash several days before the event so customers can plan ahead. Ask for your parents' support, and again, make sure to let everyone know where the proceeds are going.

Try a garage sale

Ask a few families on your block or in your neighborhood if they will donate old toys, clothes, books, furniture, and other things to your cause. Ask your neighbors for their input when setting your prices. Again, make sure to let everyone know where the proceeds will go. Remember to send those neighbors who contributed their belongings and their time thank-you notes. Turn your efforts into an annual event.

Involve the community

Ask the local store owners in your area to donate goods and services—a coupon for a manicure, dinner for two, a pair of running shoes—and host an auction. An adult can help you with the event. Have guests bid on each item. This is a great way to get the local stores in your area involved in your cause.

Sing and dance

Have you and your friends ever thought of putting on a variety show? Now's your chance. Ask a parent to be the director and the producer, and put together a few acts. Ask permission to use a public space for your production. Charge admission and let your audience know where all the proceeds will be going.

Give with your head and your heart

Before you give money to a specific charity, do your research. There are, unfortunately, some phony organizations out there. They don't do as much good for people as they should with the money they get. A good part of what they take in may go right into their pockets or into sending out more requests for donations. Beware, too, of charities that claim you have won a prize (or a family member has) but can only get information if you agree to make a donation.

Always ask for information about the charity before you donate. Once you've identified the charity that you like, you can request its annual report. The report will summarize the organization's achievements and will give you a detailed account of how it spends its money.

Young people from all over the world have worked in unique ways to raise money for many charities and help organizations, especially during emergencies and national disasters such as floods or droughts. Young people can be very powerful, successful, and strong when they work together toward a common goal.

The United States has more than nine hundred thousand charities. Whether you want to give money to build homes for people who are poor, find cures for diseases, or protect endangered children, there is something for everyone.

Here are some organizations to get you started:

Advancement Via Individual Determination:	www.avid.org
Big Brothers Big Sisters of America:	www.bbbs.org
Boys & Girls Clubs of America:	www.bgca.org
Campaign for Tobacco-Free Kids:	www.tobaccofreekids.org
Canines for Disabled Kids:	caninesforkids.org
Court Appointed Special Advocates for Children:	www.casaforchildren.org
Children's Defense Fund:	www.childrensdefense.org
Cancer Intervention and Surveillance Modeling Network:	cisnet.cancer.gov
Charities Aid Foundation:	www.cafamerica.org
Kaboom!:	https://kaboom.org
Make-A-Wish:	wish.org
Locks of Love:	www.locksoflove.org
March of Dimes:	www.marchofdimes.org
My Stuff Bags Foundation:	www.mystuffbags.org
Partnership for Drug-Free Kids:	www.drugfree.org
Save the Children:	www.savethechildren.org
Reach Out & Read:	www.reachoutandread.org

YOUR MONEY SENSE

Learning to manage money well takes time. It's not a skill that can be learned in a few hours. It takes practice. It takes discipline, perseverance, and consistency. It helps to have family and friends who can help support and encourage you in your smart money-making decisions.

Smart money-managing skills make you feel good. This is true for people of all ages. It is difficult to feel good about yourself and the world around you if you are always worried about money. If you can make smart decisions about money, you will learn to make meaningful choices in your life instead of being forced into situations because you are financially dependent on a job or a person or a place.

Making intelligent choices about money will teach you to be happy with who you are and what you have instead of always wanting more. Imagine how happy we would all be if we could be content with what we have. Good luck, young money managers! Here's to a life of smart money choices.

If you've learned anything from this book, it's that having money smarts means that you think before you spend, you carefully plan your savings, and you are consistent in your money choices. It also means that you are disciplined and creative in the way you think about things that affect your wallet. You may find innovative ways to turn your computer skills or cooking talents into cold, hard cash. Or you may invest a chunk of your savings in stocks and bonds.

THE MIND-OVER-MONEY TEST

Here's a chance to test your newly found money knowledge. Don't sweat it if your score shows that you snoozed during a few sections of this book; just go back and review anytime you need to. It's never too late or too early to polish up your money skills. And there's sure to come a time when you'll be glad you did. So, let's get started:

1. **If you get wise about money, you may be . . .**

   a. setting money goals and developing a plan to help realize those goals.

   b. earning, saving, spending, investing, and donating your money.

   c. investing all your money in that hip new restaurant chain.

   d. a and b.

2. **Anyone can make a mistake with money. The important thing is to . . .**

   a. learn from the experience.

   b. try harder to be the smartest consumer you can be.

   c. save all your receipts for a time and keep track of your spending.

   d. all of the above.

3. **Situations dealing with money and friends or family can get sticky. When money problems come up, it's best to . . .**

a. sweep them under the rug.

b. avoid spending money for two weeks.

c. talk about money issues right away to prevent bad feelings from surfacing.

d. a and c.

4. **Some things you need; some things you want. It's okay to want things, but limit them and make sure you . . .**

a. can separate your needs from your wants.

b. reward yourself every once in a while.

c. can say no to yourself.

d. all of the above.

5. **You know you're an allowance ace if . . .**

a. you put it all in the bank, even if that means you have to mooch off others to get what you need.

b. you put half of it toward snacks and drinks and the other half toward movies and music.

c. you save one-fourth of it, spend one-fourth of it, donate one-fourth of it to charities or use it for friends' birthday gifts, and put one-fourth of it into your piggy bank for lunch money and snacks.

d. you use one-third of it at the beginning of the week, one-third of it in the middle of the week, and one-third of it at the end of the week.

6. **A not-smart way to save money would be to . . .**

a. buy your lunch in the school cafeteria every day.

b. swap music, movies, and books with friends.

c. check out secondhand stores.

d. clip coupons for items you and your family use.

7. **Wise spending is . . .**

a. taking a wad of cash to the mall and making sure you spend it all in one place.

b. going to your favorite store and making sure you buy at least one thing.

c. comparison shopping at a few stores to find the best value and overall best buy.

d. buying everything you can carry from your local discount store.

8. **The very first step in setting up a budget is to make up . . .**

a. a list of everything you have ever wanted or needed.

b. a list of all your income sources.

c. a list of possible ways to cut corners when it comes to spending on others.

d. all of the above.

Your score

For each correct response, give yourself 2 points. A perfect score is 16 points. Here are the answers:

1. d 2. d 3. c 4. d 5. c 6. a 7. c 8. b

Your scorecard

0–4 points

Wake up! It's time to start thinking about money. Make a pact with yourself: think about money—ways to make it, save it, spend it, and share it—for twenty minutes a day. Take a trip to your local savings bank and watch all the action.

6–12 points

When it comes to your money skills, there's room for improvement, but don't sweat it; it's never too late to start. Learn five practical money tips a week and share them with your friends. Discuss the family budget with your parents.

14–16 points

Wow! When it comes to money sense, you are on top of things. Give yourself a hand. You really understand how money makes the world go 'round!

WHAT YOUR ANSWERS MEAN:

1. Being wise about money means you've got a plan. It also means that you are dividing your earnings into these categories: savings, spending, investing, and donating.

2. When you make any mistake, the best thing to do is to learn from it. Combine that with smart consumerism and good record keeping, and money smarts are sure to follow.

3. Talk it out. Most yucky feelings come back to haunt you when you sweep them under the rug. Being money smart means you're not afraid to discuss money matters and you're always looking for fair solutions.

4. Here's a recipe for money success: separate needs from wants, reward yourself now and again, and say no to yourself occasionally.

5. Think of your allowance as a pizza pie. Make sure to cut slices for savings, spending, charities, and presents. Also, make sure you cut a slice for transportation and snacks. The pizza will taste better that way!

6. Buying your lunch each day in the school cafeteria is definitely going to run you some bucks. Just imagine the savings if you could bring peanut butter and jelly sandwiches to school three times a week.

7. Shop around. That's the smartest advice any shopper can give or get.

8. The very first step in making a budget, before you do anything else, is finding out how much money you are bringing in. Then you will be able to tailor your wants and needs based on your income. The person bringing in $100 a week is going to have different wants and needs than the person bringing in $10 a week.

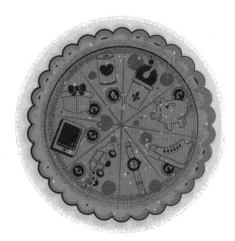

Afterword
Thoughts About Money

People don't always think it's OK to talk about money with others. But sometimes, it's good to find out how other people think about and deal with money. Here are some kids' thoughts about the green stuff:

"I don't have any money of my own. I don't need money. When I see something I like, I tell my dad I want it. If my dad says it's not too expensive, I get it."
—Ava, 7

"I'm going to be a lawyer. They make a lot of money. Then I won't have to worry about money."
—Matthew, 11

"I want to help pay for my college education. Whenever I get some money, I put it in the bank. I like knowing that I am working toward a goal."
—Maya, 12

"My first car will be a beat-up piece of junk. My second car will be really nice. The people who are my friends when I have my beat-up car will be my true friends, and they will love driving around with me in my nice car."
—Mateo, 10

"I like money. I know about bitcoin, and I am learning to trade it. I think bitcoin is the way of the future."
—Patrick, 11

Maybe some of those statements are similar to things you would say. But how do thoughts about money change once you get older? Not all adults are smart with their money. Some make lame investments, and others are just big spenders. Here are comments from a few grown-ups who have strong opinions about money:

"It's like Mom used to say: 'Do what you love and the money will come later.' I haven't made too much money, but I have loved having my summers off. You can't put a price on that."
—Anna, 36, teacher

"I wish I could have been more of a saver as a kid. It would have helped me with my finances now. I'm always scrimping and saving for something."
—Peri, 43, film editor

"I have always liked nice things and have worked hard to buy them. That's just the way I am."
—Bill, 62, dentist

"I wish I understood then what I understand now. Wasting money is just foolish. As a younger person, I always wanted the newest model. As an older person and a parent, I look for value."
—Carmita, 43, sales manager

"Credit card debt is the worst feeling ever. Be smart and don't buy on credit anything more than you have to."
—Marvin, 38, unemployed

"I wish I had majored in something in college that would have helped me land a high-paying job, like science or math."
—Nikki, 28, retail sales

"I never had much money as a kid. When I started making it as a young adult, I didn't know how to handle it. I'm just not good with money."
—Rolf, 43, plumber

"Save for a rainy day. That's the most important piece of advice I could give you."
—Steve, 52, systems analyst

You can see that everyone has different ideas and makes different choices about money. What's important is to talk about it—with your parents, with your teachers, and with your friends. Those conversations, combined with the knowledge from this book, should put you on the path to having a great relationship with money!

Additional Reading

HIP POCKET CHANGE

A site for kids from the US Mint, with games and facts about America's currency.

https://www.usmint.gov/kids/

MONEY TALKS

A University of California–run website for tweens and teens about being smart with money.

http://moneytalks4teens.ucanr.edu/

KIDS.GOV

A government website with games and videos that teaches kids how to save and spend smartly.

https://kids.usa.gov/money/index.shtml

MONEY AS YOU GROW

An initiative of the President's Advisory Council on Financial Capability, this website has different sections for kids of different ages.

http://moneyasyougrow.org/

WHERE'S GEORGE?

A fun site that tracks where your dollar bill has been!
http://www.wheresgeorge.com/

THE MINT.ORG

Run by Northwestern Mutual, a financial services company, this website has great resources for earning, saving, spending, and giving.
http://www.themint.org/kids/

Index

About the Author

JAMIE KYLE MCGILLIAN is a freelance writer who works as an editor for *Westchester Parent*. She is the author of *Pieces of Lace*, a young adult novel, as well as *The Busy Mom's Book of Preschool Activities* (Sterling). She, her husband, and their two daughters, Bailey and Devan, earn, save, spend, invest, and donate in Westchester, New York.